Monkey Jack
and
Other Stories

Palmer Cox

Hawk Press

Published by

Hawk Press
4836/24, Ansari Road, Daryaganj
New Delhi – 110 002
Phones : 9643330713, +91-11-23278618, +91-11-35676207
E-mail: thehawkpress@gmail.com
www.thehawkpress.com

MONKEY JACK

A lit-tle maid weeps pit-e-ous-ly,
    In dire dis-tress de-mand-ing aid;
Her pre-cious ball is up a tree,
    And ev-ery boy shrinks back a-fraid.

It hangs a-loft, a shin-ing thing,
    Caught by the ve-ry top-most spray,
Where slen-der branch-es ta-per-ing
    'Neath the light bur-den move and sway.

Hur-rah! he comes whom all ad-mire,
    Whose nim-ble legs, and lis-som back,
And read-y pluck, that naught can tire,
    Win him the name of "Mon-key Jack."

See how he leaps from bough to bough
    To gain that most be-lov'd of balls!
His out-stretch'd hand has caught it now;
    The branch gives way--the he-ro falls!

The fright-en'd chil-dren ut-ter cries,
    But e-ven yet he does his best;
His vic-tor hand re-tains the prize,
    And clasps it to his faith-ful breast.

Laid on his bed, com-pos'd, though sad,
    With bro-ken leg and in-jured back,
We find a lit-tle pa-tient lad,
    A-las, no long-er "Mon-key Jack!"

With books and toys, what-e'er is best,
    His com-rades seek him, one and all,
And shy-ly peep-ing through the rest,
    Poor lit-tle Ro-sa brings her ball.

Placed at the win-dow, day by day,
    While pil-lows raise his wea-ry head,
His wist-ful eyes be-hold the play
    Which once with joy-ous heart he led.

And in his hand the ball is laid,
    And if to fling it is his whim,
The sig-nal is at once obey'd,
    With ea-ger feet they run to him.

But more than this they glad-ly do--
    Each coin they get they save with care,
And Ro-sa brings her six-pence, too,
    To swell the splen-did treas-ure there.

Mon-ey can pur-chase any-thing.
    The hap-py chil-dren send to town,
And to the crip-ple's bed they bring
    A sur-geon of the first re-nown.

Oh, beau-ti-ful tri-um-phant day!

　　When light of heart and free from pain,

The pa-tient lad has slipped away,

　　And "Mon-key Jack" climbs trees again!

Here are a num-ber of lit-tle tots, and what do you think they are do-ing? I think the lit-tle girl on her knees is pay-ing for-feits.

A PAIR OF FRIENDS

Tab-by and Rover are very good friends, so that she is not at all a-fraid to eat out of his dish when-ev-er she has not din-ner e-nough of her own.

A RAIN-Y DAY

Rain, rain, rain! How it did rain! The great drops ran down the glass in streams. Tom, Jack, and lit-tle Meg watched it for a long time. "O dear!" they said at last, "do you think it will nev-er clear? We want to go out and play."

"Why do you not go up to the gar-ret, and play?" asked their mam-ma.

That struck them as a fine plan; and off they trooped, pound-ing up the bare stairs with their nois-y feet. They found three old brooms, and be-gan to play soldier,--Tom first, then Jack, with Meg las: of all. The gar-ret was ver-y large; and their mam-ma could hear them as they tramped a-long, and could hear Tom's com-mand to right a-bout face when they had reached the farth-er end.

By and by they tired of play-ing sol-dier; and then they pulled down some old dress-es and hats that hung on a peg, and put them on, and made be-lieve that they were grown peo-ple. Then, out of an old box, they dragged a scrap-book full of pic-tures, and sat them down to look them o-ver.

Mean-time their friend Rose had come, all wrapped up, through the rain, to make them a call. She brought a bas-ket, in which were her two kit-tens.

"The chil-dren are in the gar-ret," said their mam-ma.

So Rose ran up to find them. She did find them; but what do you think?--they were fast a-sleep.

Sweet is the voice that calls

From bab-bling wa-ter-falls

    In mead-ows where the down-y

        seeds are fly-ing,

And soft the breez-es blow,

And ed-dy-ing come and go,

    In fad-ed gar-dens where the

        rose is dy-ing

THE QUARREL

Grace and Bell have had a quar-rel. Bell was most at fault, but now she is ver-y sor-ry for what she has done. So she kiss-es her sis-ter, and the trou-ble is all o-ver.

OLD WINTER

Old Win-ter is com-ing; a-lack, a-lack!
    How i-cy and cold is he!
He's wrapped to the heels in a snow-y white sack;

The trees he has lad-en till read-y to crack;
He whis-tles his trills with a won-der-ful knack,
    For he comes from a cold coun-tree.

A fun-ny old fel-low is Win-ter, I trow,
    A mer-ry old fel-low for glee:
He paints all the no-ses a beau-ti-ful hue,
He counts all our fin-gers, and pinch-es them too;
Our toes he gets hold of through stock-ing and shoe;
    For a fun-ny old fel-low is he.

Old Win-ter is blow-ing his gusts a-long,
    And mer-ri-ly shak-ing the tree:
From morn-ing to night he will sing us his song,
Now moan-ing and short, now bold-ly and long;
His voice it is loud, for his lungs are so strong,
    And a mer-ry old fel-low is he.

Old Win-ter's a rough old chap to some,
    As rough as ev-er you'll see.
"I with-er the flow-ers when-ev-er I come,
I qui-et the brook that went laugh-ing a-long,
I drive all the birds off to find a new home
    I'm as rough as rough can be."

A cun-ning old fel-low is Winter, they say,--
        A cun-ning old fel-low is he:
He peeps in the crev-i-ces day by day,
To see how we're pass-ing our time a-way,
And mark all our do-ing from so-ber to gay;
        I'm a-fraid he is peep-ing at me!

THE HARD LESSON

"I can nev-er, nev-er learn it," said Bell; and she burst in-to tears.

"Car-rie has learned it," said Miss Gray; "and I am sure you can. Try, try a-gain."

"Yes, Bell," said Car-rie; "and then per-haps we can have a romp in the hay-field. You will have to hur-ry, for the men are cart-ing it in-to the barn."

Thus urged, Bell made a fresh ef-fort; and soon the les-son was learned and re-cit-ed.

Off scam-pered the two girls to the hay-field. Soon Miss Gray fol-lowed, but there was noth-ing to be seen of them. She looked all a-bout, and at last walked up to the man who was load-ing the hay on the cart.

"Can you see an-y thing of two lit-tle girls from where you are?" she asked.

"I don't see them," he an-swered, stand-ing up and look-ing a-round.

Miss Gray turned a-way, when all at once she heard a laugh be-hind her. She looked back, and there were the laugh-ing fa-ces of Bell and Car-rie. They had been on the cart, all hid-den un-der the hay in or-der to play a lit-tle joke on Miss Gray. Then they scram-bled down, and came run-ning to her.

The man on the cart smiled to see their fun. Then he said sadly, "Dear me, I wish my lit-tle lass could run a-bout like that."

"Is she ill?" asked Car-rie.

"Yes,' said the man; "but she is get-ting bet-ter now."

"We'll ask mam-ma to take us to see her," said Bell.

The ver-y next day their mam-ma did take them. They found Ruth sit-ting pil-lowed up in a chair, ver-y pale and white. Bell had picked her a bunch of flow-ers, which she seemed ver-y glad to get; and the three girls soon be-came good friends. Car-ree found a lit-tle gray kitten with which she played.

The vis-it seemed to do Ruth a great deal of good; for a pink flush came in her cheeks, and she e-ven laughed, which her moth-er said she had not done before for weeks.

They came a-gain the ver-y next day. Miss Gray was with them, and car-ried a bas-ket on her arm in which were some dain-ties to tempt the sick girl's ap-pe-tite. She was glad to see them, and told them they should have the kit-ten for their ver-y own. So pus-sy went back in the bas-ket which had brought the dain-ties.

Near-ly ev-er-y day af-ter this the chil-dren went to see Ruth, for at least a week. By that time she was well e-nough to be out, and some-times came to see them.

What is it that these lit-tle tots are all so anx-ious to see? It must
be a Christ-mas-tree.

ROB JACKSON'S DOG

Rob Jack-son's dog jumped off the lit-tle bridge in-to the mill pond to fetch a stick that Hal Jones threw for him. The wheel was in full mo-tion, and Jack, for that was the dog's name, was drawn in toward it. Rob was a-fraid that Jack was go-ing to be drowned and was just a-bout to jump in af-ter him, when one of the mill hands held him fast. "Wait a bit," said the man, and he held out a long pole to Jack who clutched it with his teeth and was drawn safely to land.

THE WIVES OF BRIXHAM

The merry boats of Brixham
Go out to search the seas;
A staunch and sturdy fleet are they,
Who love a swinging breeze;
And before the woods of Devon,
And the silver cliffs of Wales,
You may see, when summers evenings fall,
The light upon their sails.

But when the year grows darker,
And gray winds hunt the foam,
They go back to Little Brixham,
And ply their toil at home.
And thus it chanced one winter's night,
When a storm began to roar,
That all the men were out at sea,
And all the wives on shore.

Then as the wind grew fiercer,
The women's cheeks grew white,
It was fiercer in the twilight.
And fiercest in the night.
The strong clouds set themselves like ice,
Without a star to melt,
The blackness of the darkness
Was darkness to be felt.

The storm like an assassin
Went on its wicked way,
And struck a hundred boats adrift,
To reel about the bay.
They meet, they crash--God keep the men!
God give a moment's light!
There is nothing but the tumult,
And the tempest and the night.

The men on shore were anxious,
They dreaded what they knew;

What do you think the women did?
Love taught them what to do!
Out spake a wife, "We've beds at home,
We'll burn them for a light:
Give us the men and the bare ground!
We want no more to-night."

They took the grandame's blanket,
Who shivered and bade them go;
They took the baby's pillow,
Who could not say them no;
And they heaped a great fire on the pier,
And knew not all the while
If they were heaping a bonfire,
Or only a funeral pile.

And fed with precious food, the flame
Shone bravely on the black,
Till a cry rang through the people,

"A boat is coming back!"
Staggering dimly through the fog,
Come shapes of fear and doubt,
But when the first prow strikes the pier,
Cannot you hear them shout?

Then all along the breadth of flame
Dark figures shrieked and ran,
With "Child, here comes your father!"
Or, "Wife, is this your man?"
And faint feet touch the welcome stone,
And wait a little while;
And kisses drop from frozen lips,
Too tired to speak or smile.

So, one by one they struggled in,
All that the sea would spare;
We will not reckon through our tears
The names that were not there;
But some went home without a bed,
When all the tale was told,
Who were too cold with sorrow
To know the night was cold.

AGRIPPA

This is the picture of a kit-ten who lived once at a farm-house. He was such a pret-ty lit-tle cat as to be made a great pet and used to trot a-bout af-ter the peo-ple like a lit-tle dog. His name was A-grip-pa and he knew it quite well.

To this farm-house came a boy and girl named Ned and Lau-ra, to spend the sum-mer. Both were fond of pets and both played so much with A-grip-pa that he grew rath-er la-zy and did not try to catch ma-ny mice.

Ned and Lau-ra were ver-y good friends, but it happened now and then that both want-ed the same thing and then, sad to say, some loud words might be heard. Ned would say, "Give me Grip-pa," and Lau-ra would an-swer, "You shan't have Grip-pa!" and Ned would say a-gain, "I will have Grip-pa," and so it would go on till some-times poor Grip-pa would run a-way. But they al-ways made up and were friends a-gain.

Grip-pa grew up a large, fine cat, and lived some years. But he was at length taken ill. He came no more to the house, but stayed in the barn and grew ver-y weak, till he could hard-ly walk. At last, one day he came walk-ing fee-bly to the house. He went in-to the kitch-en, then to the pan-try, then to the din-ing room. In-to all the rooms went Grip-pa, and in each room sat down and looked a-round, as if tak-ing a last fare-well; then slow-ly walked out of doors. It was in-deed his last vis-it. Next morn-ing poor Grip-pa was found dead.

FRANK'S BOY

Frank More had been out skat-ing near-ly the whole af-ter-noon, for there was no school this week, and the ice was in fine or-der. It was al-most dark, and he was go-ing home, skates in hand, when a poor boy a-bout as large as him-self came up and be-gan to beg from him.

'Go home with me," said Frank, "and you shall have some sup-per."

The boy went glad-ly, and on the way Frank asked him ma-ny ques-tions. When they ar-rived, Frank took him to the kitch-en, where Jane the cook gave him a warm seat and plen-ty of sup-per, for his thin face made her feel sor-ry.

When Frank had seen him com-fort-a-bly set-tled, he went up stairs to tell his fa-ther and moth-er a-bout the lad.

'Don't you think, fa-ther," he said, "that grand-pa would like such a boy? He says he will be glad to work, and if moth-er will let me give him my old suit, I can take him to see grand-pa in the morning."

'Well, Frank, you may try," said his fa-ther. So poor Sam had a good bed to sleep in that night, and next morn-ing the two boys went to see a-bout work for him. Dressed in the warm clothes Frank's moth-er gave him, he looked like quite a dif-fer-ent boy, and was ve-ry grate-ful for her kind-ness.

It was soon set-tled that Sam should live at old Mr. More's. He had a good ma-ny things to do: to help take care of the chick-ens, the sheep and lambs, the cows and horses; and be-sides all this, he went to school, and with all the other boys, had great fun at coast-ing and skat-ing when school was out. But he worked as well as he played, and proved so trust-y, that grand-ma said: "Frank's boy was a boy worth hav-ing."

So Sam found a good home and Frank had the pleas-ure of know-ing that he had helped one boy to be both use-ful and hap-py.

JOEY'S EXPLOIT

Jo-ey Hart was a boy who was sent by his fath-er to spend the sum-mer with an un-cle in the coun-try. Jo-ey had been ill, and the doc-tor said that there was noth-ing like coun-try air to make him well a-gain.

So he set off one bright morn-ing, and be-fore night was safe at his un-cle's farm. His pa-pa had thought that Jo-ey might go to school dur-ing the sum-mer, but when the doc-tor heard of it he said no. "Let the boy run wild for three months. He will learn twice as fast next win-ter."

He was wild with joy when he was at last at his un-cle's. He was so hun-gry, and the bread and but-ter and milk tast-ed so nice-ly, that he thought he should nev-er have e-nough. Each day he was up with the sun, and by night had played so hard that al-most be-fore it was dark he was read-y to go to bed.

It was great fun to watch the men in the fields at work. Some-times his un-cle let him ride the mow-ing ma-chine, and at such times he was ve-ry proud. Then it was ve-ry ex-cit-ing to ride on the top of a great sway-ing load of hay, right in on to the barn floor.

La-ter on, when the hay was all gath-ered, the wheat be-gan to rip-en, and the men were bu-sy cut-ting it and gath-er-ing it in-to sheaves. The birds act-ed as if they thought it was cut for them on-ly, for they came in such swarms that it looked as if they would eat it all and leave none for the farm-er.

Some-times his aunt would ask him to take their lunch-eon to the men at work in the fields, for dur-ing hay-ing and har-vest when the work is heav-i-est the men al-ways have a lunch at ten in the morn-ing.

Now on one day when Jo-ey took his bas-ket and left the house for the fields, he got him-self in-to trou-ble, and this was the way. Close by his un-cle's house on the main street lived a gen-tle-man who had a fine gar-den. All a-round it was a high fence and a no-tice was post-ed up, "Tres-pas-sers will be pros-e-cu-ted." That no-tice was be-cause the school house was not far a-way, and the boys some-times helped them-selves to the old gen-tle-man's ap-ples.

Jo-ey had to pass di-rect-ly by the gar-den wall, and it so hap-pened that his bas-ket was heav-y and he set it down to rest.

What took place you can see in the pic-ture on the next page bet-ter than I can tell you. Jo-ey got the ap-ples but a bad fall, and when he went to get up he found that he could not stand and that one an-kle hurt him se-vere-ly.

How long he would have staid there I can not tell, had not the men in the field grown hun-gry and sent one of their num-ber to see what had be-come of their lunch.

The mes-sen-ger found Jo-ey, and picked him up and car-ried him home.

Then, com-ing back, he took the bas-ket and all the ap-ples that lay a-bout, and went back to the field and the men ate them all for lunch-eon.

And so Jo-ey not on-ly got no ap-ples but had to lie in bed for a week be-fore his an-kle got well e-nough for him to run a-bout a-gain.

"Oh, I say! and pippins too!!"

"I'll help myself to some of these, see if I don't Mister Notice."

Joey helps himself to more than he intended.